LIFE AS A
DAYMAKER

Lead a life that influences the world around you
by simply making someone else's day!

David Wagner

JUUT Press
Minneapolis, Minnesota

JUUT Press
201 S.E. Main Street, Suite 324
Minneapolis, Minnesota 55414

For more information call:
1-800-450-2815 or visit www.juut.com

Published by JUUT Press
Minneapolis, Minnesota 55414
First Printing 2001
Second Printing 2002

Library of Congress Cataloging-in-Publication Data

Wagner, David
Life as a Daymaker: Lead a life that influences the world around you
by simply making someone else's day

David Wagner cm.

ISBN 0-9715934-0-x (pbk.)
1. Daymaker. 2. Motivational 3. Self-help I. Title
TXu 933-298

Printed and bound in the United States

Acknowledgments

I am deeply moved by the care, support, and nurturing that was bestowed upon me throughout the process of writing this book.

I express special thanks to the many people who have brought about this dream of tipping the scales within our lifetime to create love, joy and harmony in the world through simple deeds done with open, loving hearts.

My wife, Charlie, for being my "way show-er". Your support and encouragement to live my truth is a blessing. Your love of life fills me up everyday.

My children, Coco and Ava, for being my teachers. Your sense of being, knowing, and unconditional love is a gift I cherish.

My parents, for living a life that guided me toward writing this book. Your principle of giving to friends and strangers alike is a great legacy that has taught me so many simple truths.

To my mentor, Horst Rechelbacher, Thank you for teaching me through your actions the values of passion, integrity and unwavering commitment to your noble purpose.

To Anz Johansen, my dear friend. Your ability to take my words and help me express them with clarity gave me many insights because it made me think deeper and clearer as to the true purpose of "Life as a Daymaker".

To each and every employee at JUUT, I feel extremely fortunate to find myself surrounded by such beautiful people each day. Your dedication to being Daymakers and the love and joy you bring to our clients and each other feeds my soul.

Last and not least, to you, the reader, I thank you in advance for coming to this book. My wish is that you will be inspired to live "Life as a Daymaker". In doing so, we can collectively create a ripple effect that will wash over humanity and create a world full of all that is good and right and true.

Introduction

Like many people, I searched for my purpose in this life for quite some time. Happily, I have found that purpose in marrying my beautiful wife, Charlie, raising two beautiful, spirited daughters, Coco and Ava and sharing an idea I call "Daymaking" with everyone I touch.

I want to leave my girls and others with an understanding of the impact they could have on society by simply caring for themselves, each other and everyone in their lives. This is what I call Daymaking. To make someone else's day is truly soul's work that benefits everyone involved. A simple act of kindness such as letting someone ahead of you in traffic or volunteering at your city's homeless shelter or something as important as saving a life feeds souls and in turn nourishes humanity. We also "refill our own bucket" every time we perform acts like these.

After the horrific events that took place on September 11th, 2001, my commitment to sharing and living this ideal deepened. Seeing and hearing about those amazing, unprecedented acts of courage by airline passengers, firefighters, police officers and the people of New York City and Washington D.C. filled us with a sense of astonishment, gratitude and a yearning to help any way we could. But how? Bringing back peace, balance and a sense of goodness can all start with Daymaking.

What is being a Daymaker? Simply that, being a day maker. It does not take a lot of effort; a Daymaker is someone who simply goes about life with a caring, compassionate manner of being that uplifts others. It makes life lighter and full of perfect moments. These are moments that occur exactly the way they were meant to happen for the highest good of all concerned. Perfect moments are not rare for the Daymaker; in fact they happen all the time. Happiness that comes from such perfect moments is inevitable for the Daymaker.

All of us, no matter our class, education, race, religion, etc., are all looking for the same thing out of life, happiness! It can come so easily, yet many have trouble finding that happiness, even those who seem to "have it all". My experience is that there are many people who have not known that 'the best' in life includes serving others, so they tend to find that real happiness eludes them. With Daymaking, I'm talking about genuinely making someone else's day! If you serve others for your livelihood, which many of us do, you should serve wholeheartedly, with a "servant's heart". This does not mean with servitude, but with true care and compassion for the well being of those you serve. Serve from the heart and give 110% of yourself to make their day. It will elevate your livelihood in doing so; I guarantee it, as long as it is thoughtful and genuine.

A brilliant example of a servant's heart can be seen in the efforts of New Yorkers trying to recover and rebuild their city. There have been firefighters, police officers, doctors and health care professionals at the scene since the very first moments after the attacks. Chefs from 5-star restaurants are serving food to the long lines of emergency personnel. There have also been immediate responses to calls for everything from gloves to blood to heavy equipment coming from every corner of America. School children as well as huge corporations have sent donations. Everybody has pitched in with their best efforts. These combined heartfelt offerings have lifted the spirit of New York City.

Part One

AWAKENING

Planting the Seeds

I have been referred to as "wise beyond my years", having an "old soul" and that I appear to possess the "wisdom of the ages". Quite honestly, I am often tripping over myself trying to be a Daymaker in my roles as husband, father, boss, friend and son. I feel blessed knowing that I am a Daymaker as often as I am, though it is not 100% of the time. I find myself to be all too human much of the time, and some days I end up being a Day-breaker. These are usually days when I have not taken the time to make my own day and don't have enough energy to be giving mine away. (This is an important key to being a Daymaker that we will touch on later.)

I am looking forward to a time when I can be a Daymaker at every possible moment. Imagine a life revolving around serving others and making their day. I feel that I have some extraordinary experiences to share with others who are as intent as I am on making their lives count by serving others.

I have been rewarded a thousand times over for living Life as a Daymaker. I have read numerous books, attended more seminars than I care to count, and traveled the world to find that inner peace so many people are seeking. I found that my answer was not in a book, seminar, or somewhere on a mountain halfway around the world. The answer was in my heart. I now feel like I am making a difference in the world every day. My interactions with people, whether they are family or strangers, have more to do with my own happiness and fulfillment than anything else.

This book is my gift to anyone longing to find his or her noble purpose in life. I have found my noble purpose; being a good husband and father and messenger. To me, being a Daymaker means changing the world in our lifetime. It is possible, you know. It doesn't take long to realize this phenomenon of cause and effect. Making everyone's day around you inevitably changes your life for the better. As you will see, life becomes full of perfect moments for the Daymaker. This is my message.

You may find that my life is familiar or unfamiliar to yours in experiences, opinions, hopes, dreams, regrets, and desires. Either way, I appreciate the opportunity to share my story and my hope for the future with you. If you find that we are common to each other, you may find hope in realizing that we can impact our world in incredible ways every day of our lives. If you find that we are not alike whatsoever, you may find peace, as I have, that people around the globe, who are so diverse, share many common needs and aspirations in their lives.

Me

I was raised in the small mid-western town of Hastings, Minnesota on a hobby farm. My father also grew up on a farm and he wanted to pass on the same life lessons to his children. I was an average student throughout school, as I took more of an interest in the people around me than in my studies. I was actually very shy, but I enjoyed observing everyday life around me and the interactions between people.

Growing up on the farm was a long way from the capitals of fashion. I remember getting haircuts from my grandmother on Sunday nights. Those nights always included homemade bread and the best sweet pickles I've ever tasted, but my haircuts were, at best, basic in nature.

Becoming a hairstylist

When I was fourteen, I went to my first hairstylist. It was like Hollywood for me; rock and roll music, beautiful women walking around, and I was at a ripe, impressionable age. That day, I knew I wanted to be a hairstylist (and I hadn't even seen the movie "Shampoo" yet.)

During high school, I took accounting classes because I knew I wanted to own a salon and I would need to know how to keep books and understand numbers. I also took art classes to further my creative skills, and for some odd reason I took a typing class, which comes in handy as I write this book. When I was ready to graduate from high school, my father sat me down to ask what I was going to do with the rest of my life. "I am going to be a hairstylist", I told him with conviction. Now, most fathers who are farmer/pipe-fitters in small mid-western towns aspire for their sons to become hairstylists, don't they? He simply said, "No, you're not. They don't make any money." And that was true in a small town in the 1970's.

I persisted with my vision and found the best beauty school in the Twin Cities, I attended the HORST EDUCATION CENTER, (now the Aveda Institute), in Minneapolis. I was eighteen years old, fresh off the farm and ready to open my own salon, or so I thought. Horst Rechelbacher, the owner, worked in the salon next door and charged $100 for a haircut. (In 1977, the average price for a hair cut and style in a salon was about $12.00.) "Not bad!" I thought. Upon graduation from cosmetology school, I was offered my first job with Horst Salons, valet parking the customers' cars, and you know what? I did it really, really well. In fact, I made more money than some of the hairstylists who worked inside. Then, I got a job in the salon, which was great, because it was November in Minnesota. This job consisted of shampooing clients and folding towels. Again, I did it really, really well. I did it well enough that Horst asked me to be his personal assistant, working along side him and catering to his clients. This is where I learned the art of hairstyling from the master. His passion for his work, his eye for beauty and making people look their best inspired me everyday that I worked with him. Horst also intrigued me with stories about the hairdressing traditions in Europe. So, before I started working on my own clientele, I decided to take my entire savings from valet parking, shampooing and assisting and go to Europe to gain experience in the industry and learn from the best.

I have never seen my mother so frightened as the day we said goodbye at the airport. Of course she had no need to worry, I had traveled with my family to Disneyworld a few years earlier. How difficult could Barcelona, Paris and London be? I have to admit I was nervous when I got off the plane in Barcelona, Spain without speaking a word of Spanish. I was so young, and full of curiosity and ambition, that I hadn't stopped to wonder if perhaps I should have learned the language. Looking back, this is the first example of how following my instincts would ultimately put me on the right path. I should have had much more trouble than I did but the ``people there were so kind and gracious. I found that smiling and nodding helped tremendously. I was able to study and work in some of the best salons in Europe. The people I met and the experiences I had were like a college education for me.

I returned to the U.S. and found myself working with Horst again excited to be back and take on new challenges. He wanted me to manage the St. Paul salon, as he had started a new business, a product line called AVEDA, which utilized pure plant and flower essences like no other products had before, and it was taking up much of his time and attention.

I will never forget walking into the salon the first day. In the chain of four salons, St. Paul had the most challenges to overcome. My training with Horst and my experiences in Europe helped me to see opportunities in my new location. I decided to do something about it. The easy part was working with the people at the St. Paul salon. They were great; they cared about their clients and themselves. So, we brought in different music, European magazines, and had a pizza and beer night while we cleaned the salon from top to bottom. That year, our salon went from last place in the company to first, and I was named stylist and manager of the year. That experience was one of the best in my professional career because we were ordinary people who achieved something extraordinary as a group. It was also the beginning of my Life as a Daymaker.

Around that time, the Vice-President of the company resigned to take another job. He was an MBA business guy from whom I had learned a lot. Horst called the managers into his office to talk about interviewing other business people for the position. He wanted to know what we needed from this person and what talents he should look for in the applicants. When it came my turn to reply I simply said, "If I were Vice-President, I would work on education, marketing and getting this place rocking!"

Two weeks later, Horst called me into his office and said, "You suggested that if you were Vice-President, you would do this and this and this?" I said, "Yes, I did". He responded, "Great, you're Vice-President." I didn't have a clue as to how to run a four million-dollar company with 120 employees, but I had learned how to attract, educate, and motivate great people. I was now having the time of my life at the age of twenty-three; making more money than I had ever dreamed of, living in a penthouse and sporting a boat on the St. Croix River. Life was grand.

My younger brother was eighteen at this time and my father asked what he was going to do with the rest of his life. He said he wanted to be a pipe fitter like him, and my father asked him, "Why don't you be a hairdresser?" Times had certainly changed on the farm. My brother went on to become an excellent pipe fitter and my father is very proud of him.

Opening a new business

1986 - I was having lunch in Uptown, Minneapolis when I saw a guy putting a FOR LEASE sign in the window across the street. If you're not familiar with Uptown, Minneapolis, it is THE corner to be on. Just like that it hit me! Between my appetizer and my pasta, I had opened my salon in my mind. Acting quickly and on instinct, I walked across the street, negotiated a terrible lease, and I was in business a few months later as SALON SALON, Inc.

It started with just three of us, a friend of mine and an employee who was fresh out of school. We did things differently to be unique in the marketplace. We started massaging client's scalp and shoulders before the shampoo and it was the highlight of the appointment for most customers. We served espresso and Perrier and played the coolest international music.

We also focused on education for our team members from the very beginning, facilitating opportunities for them to learn from master stylists, provided them with on-going, up-to-date training, and always fostered an atmosphere of lifelong learning. We became very busy and hired more students from beauty school and trained them in our own way. Of course, all of this hiring and training was very expensive, so I sold the boat, moved into a studio apartment and paid myself $14,000 dollars a year for the next three years while I built the business. Those were lean years in a lot of ways; working long hours and making a lot of sacrifices, but professionally, I was learning and growing immensely and laying the foundation for my place in the salon community.

After the third year, we were busy and running out of space, so I consulted a real estate broker to help me with my next move. When he asked where I wanted to expand, I told him, "I want to be right next to the Horst Salons." "Why would you want to be there?" he inquired. "That's where the customers are", I replied. "If you want to go duck hunting, you go where the ducks fly." It wasn't long before Horst heard that I wanted to expand. He called and explained that AVEDA was really taking off for him and he needed someone to run his salons. Horst taught me so much about following your own path and living a purposeful life, that I consider him not only a mentor but a "way show-er". In 1989, we merged our salon companies, and in 1991, I bought him out of the partnership. Since then, we have expanded to nine locations in the Twin Cities and bought a salon in Palo Alto, California called Yosh, from a dear friend of mine, Yosh Toya, who was retiring to travel and teach hairdressing around the world.

JUUT

After much thought, I decided to change the name of our company from Horst in the Twin Cities and Yosh in Palo Alto. Both were great, well respected brand names in their areas, yet we had grown to mean so much more to our communities, our clients, and our employees than was represented in a name, whether it was Horst, Yosh, or David for that matter. I hired an ad agency, as this is not a project to take lightly. We conducted focus groups with customers and employees. We looked at trends in the beauty and wellness industries. And we spent countless hours searching for our new name as we went through twenty two hundred possibilities. During this time, our clients kept telling us the same thing. One woman described the essence of our company particularly well when she said, "I give and I give and I give, to my family, my work, and to my friends. Here, at this salon, I get it back, so that I can go and give it away again." (This truly is the foundation of being a Daymaker) Another women described it as "having her bucket filled up." We searched for a name that meant "to refill" and we found the Japanese word "Juuten". We shortened it to "Juut" and discovered that when used as a first name, it means to uplift humanity and serve others. That was it! We named the company JUUT because it so easily describes what we do and why. Currently, we employ over 400 staff members/Daymakers and were voted one of the top twenty salons in the country.

The reason I like to share this story is because I believe that you can make a difference in any job or position you find yourself in, and that if you choose to make a difference, others will notice. I think that if I didn't park cars really, really well, I would not have gotten my inside job of shampooing and folding towels. Had I not done that really, really well, I would not have been chosen to be Horst's assistant and gone to Europe. Had I not gone to Europe, I would not have been able to make the changes in the St. Paul salon. Had I not made those changes, I would not have become the manager of the year. If I would not have become the manager of the year, I doubt I would have become the vice-president at twenty-three. Had I not had that experience, my business would not have done as well as it did and I would not have been invited to be Horst's partner and subsequently take over the company. So you see? I believe that part of the success I experience today is because I parked cars really, really well.

"Where ever you are, be there," and "Be there before you're there and someday you will be" are two of my favorite sayings.

Part Two

CLARITY

Discovering Potential

Realizing I was a "Daymaker"

Part of my career as a hairdresser included traveling and doing demonstrations around the country. When I would go to do a hair show, I usually wore leather pants, rock and roll hair, etc. I looked like one of the guys from REO Speedwagon.

On one occasion, I had just finished with a show and was traveling home. I boarded the plane and was fortunate enough to be seated in first class. I sat next to a businessman dressed in a conservative suit, neat haircut, and shiny wingtips. He looked at me oddly as I sat down next to him. I think he wondered if I knew I was in the wrong section of the plane. Surely, I wouldn't be flying first class at my age, and certainly not dressed like this. The flight got under way and he resigned himself to the fact that he would be sitting next to me for the next few hours.

I was going through the seminar I had taught earlier that day. I had described to about 800 attendees the importance of not only doing great haircuts and colors, but how we also needed to strive to make the day of everyone who comes into our salons. Just then, the businessman decided to strike up a conversation by asking me what I did for a living. "I'm a Daymaker," I replied. "What in the world is a Daymaker?" the businessman asked. "I make people's day," I said with a smile. "You must do it very well," he concluded, apparently referring to my first class seat. I went on to tell him that I was a hairdresser, but that the reason why I "did hair" was to make my client's day. He "got it" and so did I. From that day, I changed my business card to read: "David Wagner - Daymaker", instead of President/C.E.O. My clientele, business, and personal life improved dramatically after I became a Daymaker in every thing I did.

The following story is one of the best examples of how Daymaking can profoundly affect someone's life.

11

1988 - I was working in the salon when one of my clients, who normally came in every five weeks like clockwork for a haircut, came into to have her hair styled for the evening. This was odd, since I had never seen her for a style in between appointments. I figured that she must have an important social engagement that evening. When she arrived, I inquired if that was indeed the case. She said, "No, I just really want to look and feel good today." So I gave her a great scalp massage and shampooed and styled her hair. During our thirty minutes together, we joked and laughed and had a great time. When I finished, she hugged me and smiled a great smile as we said goodbye.

It was a few days later that Daymaking pierced my soul. I received a letter from this same woman, who was in the hospital.

She explained that she had come in to have her hair styled because she was planning to commit suicide and wanted to look good for her funeral. She shared with me that she had such a great time during our appointment that she left the salon, went home, called her sister and asked her to take her to the hospital to get some help. She wanted to live. She went on to thank me just for being there and caring, without having any idea what she was going through.

I often think how easy it would have been for me to have been pre-occupied that day and taken that appointment for granted, to not be there. It could have produced dramatically different results in both our lives. I thank her for the gift she gave me in that letter and that experience. It has truly shaped my life's work and me.

Now you can see the difference we can make in others' lives, whether it is something as profound as this or as simple as smiling at a stranger.

Being a hairstylist, I am constantly asked when introduced to someone, what would I do with his or her hair? The best advice I can give on beauty, I learned from Audrey Hepburn. One of my clients came upon this and took the time to send it to me. Her note said "David, this is something you have always intuitively known and shared with me without knowing you were."

Beauty Tips
by Audrey Hepburn

"For attractive lips,
Speak words of kindness.

For lovely eyes,
Seek out the good in people.

For a slim figure,
Share your food with the hungry.

For beautiful hair,
Let a child run his fingers through it once a day.

For poise,
Walk with the knowledge you'll never walk alone.

People, even more than things, have to be restored, renewed, revived, reclaimed and redeemed. Never throw out anybody.

Remember: if you ever need a helping hand, you'll find one at the end of your arm. As you grow older you will discover that you have two hands. One for helping yourself, and one for helping others."

She made my day by sending this great poem to me, and for acknowledging me for understanding it.

Why should there only be random acts of kindness? Why not totally conscious acts of kindness and good will? I believe fully that if we live our lives with the intent of being Daymakers in every thing we do, we will not only change our own lives, but the lives of everyone around us. In fact, I believe this can have a powerful ripple effect. If I touch ten customers in a day and make their day, they may go on to touch ten others in the same way. Now, I have touched not ten, but one hundred people.

We must not take this for granted! How many people do you see in a day? We have an opportunity to tip the scales of loneliness and suffering, of negative energy and harmful influences in every person we encounter.

Most everyone can relate to Daymaking. It simply starts with one small gesture on behalf of anyone in society. This ripple effect has no boundaries, racial, religious, economic or otherwise. We simply influence the world around us in a positive way. Imagine a world where we put the needs of others first, and contribute to their happiness. What goes around comes around.

If we change our negative thoughts, opinions, and emotions into nurturing, loving thoughts and actions, we can literally change our world. There is a spiritual revolution occurring where people, including myself, are becoming more aware and committed to a world full of love, light, joy, and abundance. Many have written about it, many more have read about it. Now it's time to take what we have learned and act on it. I love the quote by Margaret Mead, "Never doubt that a small group of thoughtful, committed citizens can change the world, indeed it's the only thing that ever has." It all has to start somewhere, why not with you, your family, your friends, and your community? It's simple, start consciously making other people's happiness part of what makes you happy, what fills you up, what makes the world a better place. I believe that I will see this in my lifetime and I invite you to help in this effort by simply making every day a joyful one by serving someone else in big or small ways.

You have not lived a perfect day until you have done something for someone without expecting them to repay you. We can experience the best in life by Daymaking.

MAKING EVERY DAY COUNT

Smile and say hello to strangers

When I am with my daughters walking down the street, I tell them we are going to wave at everyone we see and wish them a good day. When you do this with a five and a two-year-old, everyone smiles and says 'thank you'. Some shake their hands and some have even hugged them. When I do this on my own, people seem entertained, amused, or just think I'm having a good day. I have not gotten a hug yet, but remain hopeful.

Send a kind clerk a note

I sent a thank you note to our local hardware store for their excellent service. The owner celebrated it with all of his employees. Most business owners only receive bad news about their staff. Take the time and make not only the employee's day, but the owner's as well. I am speaking from experience. I appreciate when customers send me a note if we have let them down, yet when someone takes the time to write or call, praising our staff and our business, it really makes my day.

Send nurses a thank you note if you or a loved one has been in the hospital

They are truly heroes in our society and we need to recognize them for it.

Read uplifting stories and share them with people

People tend to focus on and share the negative news in the world. 'Did you see in the paper?' 'Did you see the news last night?' I met a guy in Maui who was working on a new cable news station called GNN, the Good News Network. The only stories they will run are positive, uplifting news events around the world. Pretty cool idea, don't you think?

Listen to great music with uplifting lyrics

Driving to work for me is like 'pre-game.' I listen to music that uplifts me and puts me in a great mood so that when I walk into work, I bring with me an energy of love and joy.

Dance in public

I went to an outdoor concert given by Taj Mahal, a great rhythm and blues, jazz-fusion artist. We were down near the stage, where a number of people were dancing. One was a little girl, about five years old. Another was a gentleman in his forties. People around me were commenting on how cute the little girl was but at the same time, were ridiculing the guy for dancing so freely in public. At what age are we supposed to stop dancing because it isn't cute? What if everyone just 'danced like no one was looking?' I admire people who dance and display this kind of freedom and security within themselves.

Loan people money

One of my favorite books is <u>The Richest Man in Babylon</u>. To loan money to someone you know is worthy of your trust helps them gain a sense of accomplishment in their lives. Many people lack the confidence it takes to get their financial life in order. Many times, paying back a small loan will give them this sense of confidence and being trustworthy.

Support local merchants

I grew up in a small town and now live in a small town. I enjoy the relationships I have with local shop owners. I could get things cheaper sometimes, quicker other times, but at the end of the day, I feel better supporting my neighbors and the tax base of my own town.

Compliment a woman who changes her hair

She'll enjoy it, and so will her hairstylist.

Let people merge into traffic

Why is it that when you let someone merge onto the highway, they turn and wave to thank you? It's because it is so rare these days. Everyone is in such a hurry to get to work, school, soccer, or home that, God forbid we make someone's day and let them merge in front of us. Why are we in such a hurry that we can't show up for work one car length later? (Note: If you let more than one person in at a time though, I've noticed that it doesn't make the day for the person behind you. Be practical, you don't need to stop, just be a Daymaker.)

Tip as much as you can

Even if it's only a little, leave something. It will make your day as much as the one receiving the tip! I received a great story that best describes this point.

In the days when an ice cream sundae cost much less, a 10 year old boy entered a coffee shop and sat down at a table. The waitress put a glass of water in front of him. "How much is an ice cream sundae?" he asked.

"Fifty cents," replied the waitress. The little boy pulled his hand out of his pocket and studied the coins in it. "Well, how much is a plain dish of ice cream?" he inquired. By now, more people were waiting for a table and the waitress was growing impatient. "Thirty-five cents," she brusquely replied. The little boy again counted his coins. "I'll have the plain ice cream," he said. The waitress brought the ice cream, put the bill on the table and walked away. The boy finished the ice cream, paid the cashier and left.

When the waitress came back, she began to cry as she wiped down the table. There, placed neatly beside the empty dish, were two nickels and five pennies. You see he couldn't have the sundae, because he needed to have enough left over to give her a tip.

Always leave a tip; it will make your day!

Remember to Make Your Own Day

How do you make your own day and fill up your own bucket? I find that in order to be uplifting, I myself have to be uplifted. There are many ways that I do this. Getting up early and simply watching the sunrise gives me incredible energy for the day. Starting the day with a yoga or meditation ritual will help you focus your energy and your intention for the day. I take immense pleasure in the little things in life that also help me to focus; my daughters' smiles, giggles, and bright eyes always remind me to be in the moment and expect wonderful things to happen.

Try to put yourself on the path of beautiful things as you start your day. Listen to the birds outside, the rain falling, become aware of all that nature has to offer. So many people start their days by watching TV or listening to negative drive time radio. We have a choice how to begin each day. Why not do it with beauty? It's easy to get out of the rut...set the alarm clock for 30 minutes earlier than usual and take that time to fill your senses and enjoy the stillness. My best work has been done on these mornings, with the least effort. It becomes easier and easier to hear things when you take the time to listen intently and quietly.

When was the last time you treated yourself to a spa day at home? I find that a great way to recharge my battery is to simply take a few hours in the evening to "bliss out." Here is a very easy way to melt stress and refill your soul. You will need the following:
- *Your favorite relaxing music*
- *Candles with a natural aroma that you love*
- *Bath salts/essential oils*
- *Massage oil*
- *Large bath robe*
- *Favorite poetry book*
- *Relaxing tea*

Sounds good already, doesn't it? Make sure that you have two hours with no interruptions. Unplug the phone, put the kids to sleep, etc. Now, run a hot bath, adding your favorite bath salts or essential oils, put on your favorite music, light the candles, pour yourself some calming tea and slide into your luxurious bath. I like to do a breathing exercise while bathing that allows me to focus on filling up my core with light through each breath. Imagine pulling light into your heart chakra each time you breathe in. Keep filling that space with more and more light. You can actually begin to see light filling up your whole being. This in itself is so relaxing.

Take the time to give yourself a great scalp massage while you shampoo your hair. Simply move around the scalp and forehead while massaging in a circular motion. Feel the sensation of stress melting away especially around the temples. When you have a sense of stress leaving your body and light filling that space, you will be calm and uplifted at the same time. It's an amazing place to be.

After your bath, use your massage oil to further relax the muscles in your legs, arms, shoulders, etc. By simply using your fingertips and breathing deeply during this ritual, you can take yourself into a deeper, calm place. Lastly, wrap yourself up in a large bathrobe, refresh your tea and find a comfortable place to read. (I am particularly fond of poetry on my own spa night.) There you go! How do you think you will feel in just two short hours? Believe me, it's more relaxing than some vacations I've been on. There is something special about being in a familiar space, (your home) and just letting go. I urge you to build your own rituals during your spa night.

"REFILL YOUR OWN BUCKET"

Take a long walk and just concentrate on your breathing.

I find it helpful to take two steps while breathing in and three steps breathing out. It forces the carbon dioxide out of the body and refills it with oxygen. This is a technique used by marathon runners for better endurance. It helps me quiet my mind.

Read a great novel

I used to spend most of my reading time focusing on business, marketing, fashion, etc, which educated me but didn't really replenish me. I still read these types of books but now I include great novels, fables, and uplifting autobiographies. I find that it takes me away from the numbing effects of the television.

Learn how to give a massage

Surprise your child, wife, parent or grandparent by offering them a massage. Even if it's just rubbing their hands or feet, it will make their day. I will never forget the day I was married. My parents and I stayed in a hotel the night before. The afternoon of the wedding, I was getting ready with my dad and he sat me down in a chair and gave me a neck and shoulder massage. We didn't say anything to each other; we just enjoyed the moment together. It is one of my fondest memories of the day.

Avoid making early appointments if it disrupts your morning rituals

I love my mornings to be as stress free as possible. Then I can enjoy some quality time for my family. My daughter has to be at school at 8:45 a.m. and I drive her everyday. The time in the car with just the two of us is a ritual in itself. Having the time to enjoy each other in the morning is important to me. I rarely schedule early meetings or appointments. I work smarter, not longer, and lead a balanced life that I'm proud of.

Unplug the TV

Ask yourself if the shows you watch each day contribute anything positive to your life. Do they boost your energy level, challenge your thinking in any way or create a sense of purpose? We own one TV and we rarely watch it. Think about the impact that repeated showings of crime, violence, and negativity have on your peace of mind and more importantly your children's minds. There are opportunities every day to teach our kids to be doers vs. viewers.

We also ask our babysitter to not utilize the TV to keep the kids occupied with mind-numbing shows and commercials. I used to be a news junkie and had all the cable channels that were available. When my kids got a bit older, I decided not to be held hostage by the T.V. any more and canceled my cable. Now I spend time with my kids, not just in the same room watching the monotonous schedule of shows.

Get out of debt!

I think that one of the most stressful things that we can do is be in over our heads financially. If you can't get through the month without a credit card, it's time to trim your budget. The key is simply to make more than you spend. It sounds so simple, but we get in our own way for several reasons I would like to address. Getting out of debt is very liberating. It allows you to replenish yourself by not being burdened with the stress that it creates. Imagine how much time, energy, and thought you could put into Daymaking if you had your debt under control.

Here are a few ideas to minimize or eliminate the stress related to debt:

- Only use one or two credit cards with interest rates that are the best your credit history will allow.
- Remember that you don't have to buy everything in the baby store to be a good parent; in fact I think you're a better parent by resisting the desire and getting further into debt.
- Think of the stress that's caused by going into debt vs. the benefit your child may feel being surrounded by new clothes or toys. I think your child would choose to have a parent who is full of love and joy and in a great mind set rather than the temporary satisfaction that purchased goods seem to give.
- Be an example for your kids by limiting your own consumption. Take joy in moments rather than things. Stay out of the mall. Invest in your future. The best book I have read on the simple principles of finance is <u>Rich Dad, Poor Dad</u>. In it, there is a simple formula for creating a comfortable retirement for yourself. Invest 10% of your income and don't touch it.
- Investing as early in your life as possible makes a huge difference. In our company, there are several staff members who started investing in their early 20's. Now, ten years into their program, they are amazed at how quickly their worth has increased. The earlier you do this, the better.
- Don't go into debt to buy Christmas presents. I would rather receive a gift that I know is from the heart, within his or her budget, and with great intention, than something frivolous and costly.

Refill your body

Nutrition is a great way to refill your bucket. Avoid processed foods by finding organic restaurants and grocery stores. Eat regularly and slowly, and drink plenty of water. Water should be our beverage of choice. When you look at most alternatives such as sodas, coffee, alcohol, etc., none of them are as good for us and they do not nourish our body. You are what you eat! How many times have we heard this, right? I have found that it has helped me immensely by paying attention to what I put into my body. Eating whole foods that are grown and prepared with good intentions gives me an energy that I just don't get from over processed foods. I enjoy going to the farmers market with my wife and children and buying food directly from the farmers and their families. We have gotten to know them and it feels good to support family farms that have chosen the organic route to farming. We have also become part of a community farm where you buy shares in their annual crop. Each week the farmer delivers whatever was harvested and delivers it to our home. The kids love being surprised by each week's harvest.

Throw out the microwave

We have done without a microwave in our house for eight years now and I don't even think about it as an option any longer. We have also incorporated this into our business and taken the microwaves out of our lunchrooms. Now our staff members are more mindful of what they eat and how it's prepared. When a person runs behind, it's great to see fellow employees help out by cooking their food for them with iron skillets. The community in the lunchroom has changed and staff members have actually enjoyed it. Like most things, after thirty days, they don't miss the microwave a bit. In fact, many have taken the new habit home to their own families.

Take up Yoga

It is the best way to quiet the mind and balance and tone the body that I know of. Everyone can benefit from some form of yoga. You can get started a number of ways, through books and videos, or classes in your community. Yoga classes are popping up everywhere. My parents live in a small Mid-western town where my mother practices it at the senior center.

(GAIAM is a great resource for yoga books, videos, props and clothing. They carry everything needed for pre-natal yoga to yoga for elderly people. Call 1-800-254-8464 or write to www.gaiam.com to request a catalog.)

Make a plan for your wild ideas

I am a fan of Zig Ziglar. About twenty years ago, I started focusing on my wild ideas. I sit down every three months and write down everything I dream of Being, Doing, and Having. Sometimes, I come up with fifty and other times, one hundred and fifty. Don't just write down easy goals, get out there, and get wild with your ideas. Over the years, I have written down: being President of the United States, driving a grand prix race car, living in the South of France, marrying the perfect woman and being a famous actor to name a few. Stretch yourself with your wild ideas. The next step is to write down in one sentence why you want to Be, Do, or Have that particular goal. I have found that this is when a lot of the frivolous ones go by the wayside. Take the goals that most articulate your desires, and put those on the top of your list. I still leave the others on my wild idea list, but not at the top. Now the next step is very important. Share your list with those who can help put you in the way of your wild ideas. The more people you share your wild ideas with, the more likely they are to occur. The odds simply multiply if there are more people looking out for you. I have shared my ideas with family, friends, co-workers, bosses, industry associates, my wife and my children.

Some of the wild ideas I have achieved that other people helped facilitate for me include traveling and speaking in Australia, skydiving, race car driving, finding a rare boat, buying companies from Horst and from Yosh, the house we live in and a host of others. My employees help me achieve my wild idea of having a great company doing great things. What I have found is that people get burnt out easily if they don't achieve big and small goals in their lives. The ways to keep yourself out of this state of burn out is to constantly be purposeful in your actions and recognize the achievements that you've made. Working hard doesn't cause burn out, not achieving something does.

Peace

The past five years have been extraordinary for me. It was during this time that I really began experiencing what I had been reading about all these years; meditation, yoga, proper breathing, the effects of nutrition and balance in my life. I was also inspired by a friend of mine named Ray Civello, who went to India when he turned 40 and spent time with the famous sages of the Himalayas. He came back a changed man. I had read a ton of books on meditation, visualization, listening to your inner guides, etc., but I realized that I hadn't really practiced any of these teachings. I saw Ray's clarity, purpose, and soul had come alive, and I understood for the first time how much I didn't know. I was not in a position with my family or my business to travel to the other side of the world to understand what he had learned. So I looked around to see what other resources were available to me in Minneapolis, Minnesota? Closer to home, I have had opportunities to meet a number of extraordinary individuals. One of them is Dr. Justin O'Brien, author of Walking with a Himalayan Master and The Wellness Tree. He is an American who has become a celebrated Swami and is based in St. Paul, Minnesota. I read about him, got to know him over the course of many years, even had him present his thoughts and philosophy to my staff. After listening to Ray's inspiring stories, I made an appointment with Dr. O'Brien and told him I wanted to see more clearly, to know what I didn't know. He chuckled, having known me over the years and said, "Ah, the student has arrived this time." We agreed to meet every Wednesday and spend a couple of hours together. For the first three months, all we did was breathe, literally. We breathed correctly and on purpose. It was quite astounding to me how quiet you can become in a short time. People started to notice my enhanced patience, understanding, clarity, and intent. All that I had been longing for was mine simply by taking the time to breathe. Shortly after learning and practicing correct breathing, I found myself meditating on a different level and noticing so much more around me.

Imagine your mind is a lake. When the water is stirred by a storm, the mud from the lake's bottom clouds it up and makes it difficult to see clearly. Much of life is a storm and our minds get clouded by all the activity and stress in everyday life. When the storm passes, the lake is clear. This is what meditation has done for me. I see clearly, once I let the lake settle. The stormier life is, the more I meditate.

I now realize my potential. What if I actually did the things I am capable of and became the person the universe intended me to be? I became so exhilarated by the whole idea that I could change the world, even if it's only my little corner. I know this is the legacy I want to leave my children. Everything else now seems so trivial in comparison. I am fortunate to have a friend in Ray, for his going to the mountain and inspiring me to receive the message of clarity, purpose, and intentional living. I expect that I will be going to India someday, yet right now I can tell you that I believe fulfillment can be achieved anywhere in the world.

Part Three

BALANCE

Roles We Play

DAYMAKER ROLES WE PLAY

The following thoughts are specific to the various roles that we play and areas in life that inspire and bewilder me. I would like to share with you how I approach these roles and subjects as a Daymaker. This would be a good time to take a moment and think about the last time that someone really made your day; this is truly the essence of the book. Take a moment to visualize what your relationships, work, and life would be like if you lived each day as a Daymaker.

- Daymaker Husband -

I feel so blessed being married to my wife. I asked her to help me with this section and let other men know what would make their wives' day. I gave her a legal pad and pen and asked her to write down ten things that I could do to be a Daymaker for her. Here is her list:

1. Listen
2. Communicate
3. Participate
4. Listen
5. Communicate
6. Participate
7. Listen
8. Communicate
9. Participate
10. Refer to 1-9

Certainly, I got the point after reading that! Those three actions top my "to do" list every day.

Marriage, I believe, is a 60/60 split. Always give 10% more than you expect. Better still, is not to expect anything in return. (I'm still working on that.) I enjoy my wife and our life together because I feel that she truly is my soul mate. Soul mates know how to push your buttons, make you think, challenge you and in the end, facilitate growth. They love you unconditionally, bumps and warts and all. I have grown immensely in my life through my marriage. I enjoy heated conversations and debates with my wife as much as the synergy and like-minded thoughts that we share. We teach each other a lot and in the process understand each other at a very deep level. My wife is my best friend, confidante, teacher and life coach. We share our love for life.

Simple Gifts

After getting married, I learned something wonderful about the art of giving. Spending a dollar on something unique and meaningful is worth more to my wife than spending fifty dollars on something expected and ordinary. On Valentine's Day a number of years ago, I was driving around trying to figure out what to buy to let her know how special she was to me and how much I love her. I walked in and out of stores without a clue as to what I was going to get her. I went to a drug store in the process to get some cough drops. There, I saw a picture in a frame of a little boy and girl kissing on the beach. I bought the picture and frame for $6.99 and went to a coffee shop to think about what I could write on the picture. I simply wrote the name Charlie on a piece of paper and thought about our life together. Here is what I gave her that evening:

Certain I would meet
Her someday, I kept looking.
All my life I knew what she would be like.
Rare as the most precious stone, yet she
Loves the little things in life, gardens, summer walks, & me.
I'm the most fortunate man I know.
Especially now with Charlie!

My poem on that picture is one of her favorite possessions. It is so easy to take for granted those who are nearest to us, and to acknowledge them with the obvious gifts that our society measures love with, yet it is so much better to find (or make) something that is from the heart, that has special meaning to you. That was the best $6.99 I have ever spent.

I heard a great description on marriage; "A successful marriage is one in which it never occurs to you that you've compromised anything."

MAKE YOUR SPOUSE'S DAY

Compliment them in public and in private

Leave love notes on the bathroom mirror to start their day

Put a love note somewhere secret, in a place where they will find it sometime during the day; briefcase, wallet, car, coat pocket, etc. They may not find it for days, but they will find it and it will make their day.

Find a video that teaches how to do massage, then, practice on each other regularly.

Send flowers anonymously, for no reason at all except the obvious, that you love them dearly.

If you have children, it's a great gift to give spouses an unplanned morning off to themselves

Start with breakfast in bed prepared by you and the kids and then go to the park for a few hours while they have an unexpected morning free.

Hold hands in public

It is a rare sight for couples who have been married for a long time. Act like you're dating even after the years have gone by.

- Daymaker Father -

Wow! What a role to play. I knew I was a grown up as soon as my first daughter, Coco, let out her first cry. It is said that you can become and not become a number of roles, but you will never not be the father or the mother of your child. They are yours to keep, care for, teach and cherish. I would like to share some of the lessons I've learned as a father, as well as some thoughts on how we can help our children fulfill all of their potential. My wife and I have been blessed with two incredible beings in our lives this time around. Our first daughter, Coco Arabella, and our second, Ava Mirabella, are five and two years old at the time of this writing. So, I am still somewhat new at this role I play called Daddy.

The lessons I've learned thus far in fatherhood have served the other areas of my life as well. The understanding, patience, compassion, and being a student of my children have all helped me to be a better boss, friend, brother, and son.

It is so important for us as fathers to get to know our children and allow them to get to know us. This incredible relationship can begin while your child is in her mother's womb. I remember talking to Coco, and how she knew my voice and responded by kicking and moving around. Take the time, it makes their day. It's also important to take care of mom during this time. Foot and back massages are gifts that you can both look forward to at the beginning or end of the day. There are some wonderful videos on pregnancy massage that will allow you both to bond with this new little being who is so anxious to meet you. My wife's friends were always envious of her, talking about our massages, baths, and rituals around her pregnancy. Go ahead make her day! Every day! All it takes is some soothing music, a little massage oil, some of your undivided attention and a couple of soothing Daymaker hands.

34

The big day...My wife gives birth to a beautiful girl! After a brief introduction to our tiny new family member, the nurses took her to be weighed, cleaned, and documented. If I can give any words of advice to dads on this segment of the birth experience, now is the time for you to be with your child. Sitting behind a glass wall video taping, like I see some fathers doing, is not the answer. Get in there, roll up your sleeves, and give your child their first hug, caress, bath, and that indescribable love you have for them the second they are born. You will not forget this unique moment for all your life and neither will they.

When my wife and child and I came home, Grandma was there, and sisters who had children were there, all helping out in their own ways. I ended up in the background somehow trying to figure out what we needed around the house, which bills needed to be paid, all the cool stuff, right? I realized I did not know anything about an infant and her needs even after all those hours of birth and parenting classes. I not only felt ill prepared, I felt unnecessary during those first few days. I tried to help, but I was still so unsure of my new roles of Daddy and husband to a woman who had just given birth, and all that those roles require. I sat one night rocking my new daughter, thinking about how I could make her day. Finally, it dawned on me, something completely obvious to someone in the wellness industry, yet it had escaped me... infant massage! So, I took her to one of our spas and had a massage therapist teach me how to work on her tiny body. I bought a how-to book (they have videos now, too) and proceeded to give Coco a massage every night at precisely the same time. It became our own special ritual that allowed me to bond with her in ways that I could not have imagined otherwise.

I was very lucky to be able to spend much of my time at home with my new family. I learned so much from and about my little girl during the first month of her life. At only a few weeks old, Coco's spirit, her will, her character, and her whole being became obvious to me. By getting to know her, I was able to find the words to celebrate her birth and her potential in life. Had I not spent the time, I simply would not have become aware. Take the time, become aware and enjoy this most precious time you have together.

The following is our first daughter Coco's Birth Announcement:
Announcing the birth of
Coco Arabella Wagner
Born to David and Charlie Wagner
On September 30th, 1996
Weighing 6lbs. 10 oz. and measuring 19 1/2 inches long.

Complete is the word most
Often in my mind when I look at her.
Children have always had me in the palms of their hands,
Ours has me to the tips of my toes and more.

Already she
Reaches out to touch the smiling faces of everyone
Around her.
Before we know it, these little hands will
Explore, discover, finger paint and play the piano.
Little hands that may someday sculpt, cut hair or heal those in pain.
Love has never meant more to me
And everyday I can only hope I'm worthy of this blessing we call Coco.

    - Her father

I am so glad that I went the extra mile in writing her announcement. I can only imagine the impact that it will have on her when she can understand how much she means to me. If anything were to happen to me, she will know that I knew her essence, her soul, and her potential. That in itself is comforting to a father.

Take the time to make their day. Let them know how they have made your day by gracing your life with theirs. Honor them by making an extra effort, it will be significant in their life and yours.

Our second daughter, Ava, came along at a time when we had just purchased a new business in Palo Alto, California and we were "full tilt boogie" in business deals, remodeling, hiring, and training new staff. So, about four months into our new highly leveraged deal, we found out we were pregnant. We were already trying to figure out how to get half way across the country with one eighteen-month old child, and now an infant.

It was difficult to give my wife the same amount of time and support with our second child, because of all of the traveling I was doing for business, but I made it a priority by giving my time and my energy. In the middle of Charlie's second trimester, we were made aware that this was going to be a different pregnancy experience altogether. During a routine test, the doctor discovered a possible abnormality and asked us to return the next day for more conclusive tests. We went ahead with the tests and found that we were at high risk for having a baby with Downs Syndrome, Spina Bifida or a combination of other birth defects.

Now, how can you possibly even try to make someone's day after experiencing something like this? Believe me, it's difficult. Sometimes silence and strength is all that you can offer. We drove home holding onto each other's hands so tightly, trying to give each other strength, wisdom and the right words to say, when a song came on sung by the Italian opera singer, Andrea Bocelli. It struck us both so deeply with its beauty that we both fell silent. That was such an important, impactful moment for us. We listened to that same song over and over, into the night, and on our way to other doctor's appointments; anytime we just wanted to share that moment. To this day, when we hear it, we cry.

We went to many subsequent meetings with Doctors and Genetic Counselors. I am convinced that they tried to prepare us for the worst and hope for the best. We were told that to have an absolutely conclusive diagnosis, they would need to perform an Amniocentesis. We gave it a lot of thought and decided that we wanted to know what we were facing. That way, we could emotionally prepare ourselves, our family, do as much research around the complications as possible, and welcome this exceptional spirit into our lives with peace and understanding.

During the Amnio, we could actually see on the monitor the needle going into Charlie's womb and our child reaching out for it with her tiny hand as to say "Hey! This is my womb!" Following that test were twelve days of incredible anxiety and extraordinary hope. The hope, support, prayers and love surrounding us from our family and friends were inspiring. I believe that it was this combined energy that got us to the point where we knew we would have the strength to deal with any outcome. I remember talking to my mom late one night and posing the question, "If not us, then who? We can handle this emotionally, spiritually, and financially. We can do this, and we will."

Twelve days later, we received the results of the Amnio. Perfectly normal! Although there could still be some unforeseen complications, it appeared that we were "out of the woods." I remember such a mix of emotions, of gratitude and relief that we would have a normal child and how blessed we were. Yet somehow,

I felt a strange sense of loss as to the lessons we would have learned from a child with special needs.

On February 20, 1999, our daughter Ava Mirabella was born perfectly normal, except for one very distinctive birthmark. She greeted us with this perfectly round mark, the size of a silver dollar, right on the crown of her head with a two inch long, pitch black crop of hair growing out of it. We were quite amazed by our "Little Buddha", and so thankful that she was otherwise healthy.

When we brought Ava home, a spiritual friend of ours held Ava and said, "Oh my! This birthmark is where God put his hand on her when you accepted her however she may be." Wow! Our child and her birthmark are so perfect in every way. In her very short life so far, she has taught me more than anyone I've ever known has. Her life has blessed ours in a way that is hard to explain. She made us understand that all life is precious beyond words, she gave us strength we never imagined we had. She made us realize the fear, anxiety, hope and most of all, unconditional love that came from this experience. I feel blessed by the lessons that she taught me before she had even taken her first breath. We had another wise little Daymaker coming into our lives!

If you are going to make one of your children's days, you absolutely must make the other child's too. Again, I took time each night and performed massage on my new daughter, and got to know her. I wanted to express my appreciation to her for the lessons she taught us and to God for placing her in our lives.

The following is our daughter Ava's Birth Announcement:

Announcing the birth of
Ava Mirabella Wagner
Born to David and Charlie Wagner
On February 20th, 1999
Weighing 7lbs. 7oz. and measuring 19 1/2 inches long.

Again I am reminded of the
Very greatest gift of all, the unconditional love of
Another

Mere words simply can't describe her will and spirit.
In God we trusted and here we are today looking into her eyes
Reveling in what we have to share with this world.
Already she inspires us to
Be all that is good and right and true.
Everyone will notice these
Lovely lips, as they will speak words of kindness, these
Lovely eyes, as they will seek out the good in all people.
And everyday I will hope I am worthy of this blessing we call Ava.

- Her father

Now that I have five and two-year old daughters, it seems as though the days have gotten so much shorter. No "me" time. Before I had children, I slept in on Sundays, read the paper and had leisurely mornings with my coffee and croissant. Those days are gone. For all of you who are parents, I'm sure you can relate. The sad thing for me was that I felt like I had lost something in giving up my Sunday mornings. I felt kind of sorry for myself, having to get up, play "chase me around the house", change diapers, and make breakfast at 6:30 a.m. on a Sunday morning. I was lucky to get to my paper or my coffee by noon, if ever.

One cool summer night, a few months after Ava's arrival, I was the keynote speaker for a graduation at a local school. A student gave a speech that night that hit me like a two by four. It rang so true to how I was feeling at the time. I felt sorry for myself with all that I was dealing with at home, in my business, and life in general. This speech not only changed my Sunday mornings; it changed my life and how I look toward every day.

Her speech went like this:

"*We convince ourselves that life will be better after we get married, have a baby, then another. Then we are frustrated that the kids aren't old enough and we'll be more content when they are. After that, we're frustrated that we have teenagers to deal with. We will certainly be happy when they're out of that stage. We tell ourselves that our life will be complete when our spouse gets his or her act together, when we get a nice car, are able to go on a nice vacation, when we retire… The truth is, there is no better time to be happy than right now. If not now, when? Your life will always be filled with challenges. It's best to admit this to yourself and decide to be happy anyway.*"

Similarly, the following is one of my favorite passages by Alfred D. Souza:

"For a long time it had seemed to me that life was about to begin - real life. But there was always some obstacle in the way, something to be gotten through first, some unfinished business, time still to be served, a debt to be paid, then life would begin. At last it dawned on me, these obstacles were life."

This perspective has helped me to see that there is no way to happiness. Happiness is the way. So, treasure every moment that you have. Treasure it more because you shared it with someone special, then, make their day!

Remember that time waits for no one, so, stop waiting until...

- you finish school,
- you lose 10 pounds,
- you have kids,
- your kids leave the house,
- you start work,
- you retire,
- you get married,
- you get divorced,
- Friday night, Sunday morning
- you get a new car or home,
- your car or home is paid off,
- Spring, Fall, Winter,
- you're off welfare,
- the first, or 15th,
- you've had a drink,
- you sober up,
- you die,
- you are born again...

to decide that there is no better time than right now to be happy.

Happiness is a journey, not a destination. I find that when I am in the moment and being a Daymaker, I experience my happiest moments, especially on those Sunday mornings with my girls.

You know how my kids spell love? It's T-I-M-E. Not only the quantity of time, but also the quality of it. Developing rituals is an important part of parenthood. Flying kites in the spring, baiting a hook to go fishing off the end of the dock, riding the bicycle, and taking long walks on the beach looking for shells are some of our favorites. You don't need to spend lots of money, it just takes time. Time is not money, like some people say it is. Time is life. I believe my children will judge me by this in the end. Make their day by giving them a part of yours. Spending a day with your children is a gift.

MAKE YOUR CHILDRENS' DAY

Don't bring work or worries home from the office.

When you walk in to greet your family, roommate, or spouse, leave the "garbage" outside Imagine if there was a hook outside your door where you could hang all your troubles and worries for the evening. What I have noticed is that when I do this, there always seems to be fewer of them when I leave the next morning.

Don't put a TV in a child's room

You can set a great example by not having one in your room.

Under promise and over deliver

I have found that I make fewer promises as a parent, so I can keep them all. This is an important point that my five-year-old coaches me on daily. Amazing, the memory of a five- year-old child

Teach your children the joy of solitude and quiet time

This will allow them time to develop their own thoughts instead of being bombarded by someone else's through TV and advertisements. You will find that they will respect your desire for quiet time as well.

Help your child with making gifts that don't have to be purchased

Teach them the value of authenticity and care in giving a poem or hand made gift to a friend, grandparent, etc. They will come to appreciate them as gifts for themselves as well.

Go to the park and participate in the fun

I used to go with the kids and watch them play. I then found that I got more out of it by becoming a child myself and playing on the monkey bars. I can tell you that my kids get more out of it as well. I try not to spend as much time in life being a spectator on the sidelines. It is much more fulfilling when I participate whether it's in activities at the park or in the kitchen with my wife.

Make a ritual of watching sunsets with your children

We are fortunate to live on a lake, so we regularly find a quiet place to just anchor and be with each other during this magical time of day. Don't have a lake? It's just as easy to set up a blanket in the back yard or your favorite park. Make a ritual out of it by using the same blanket.

Keep a diary for your children

Every year I'm amazed at how many things, large and small, I have forgotten about our children's daily experiences. I decided when Coco was turning one, that I would write her a letter on her birthday to recount the year for her. I shared the things she taught me, how much I love her and what she's added to my life. I now write a letter on each birthday my daughters celebrate. I put the letter in a special envelope, seal it and put it in our safe. I intend to give them their letters on their eighteenth birthdays. I pray I am around to be there when they read them, and if I'm not, I will have the comfort of knowing they know how I felt about them growing up and the life we've shared.

Create traditions in your life around Daymaking

Helping prepare Thanksgiving Day food for the poor, caroling, helping dad put the dock in at the lake, Fourth of July barbecues. All of these traditions have a lasting impression, especially on kids. When I was single, one of my traditions was to go shoot pool with my Dad on Christmas Eve Day. My brothers were both married and spent that day with their in-laws then came to my parent's house on Christmas day. My Mom was always preparing for Christmas on this day, so she was grateful to have us out of her hair. These afternoons of shooting pool and having a few beers with my dad at the local VFW are some of the most memorable times I've had with him. It was just the two of us, hanging out being buddies. We did this for years, until I got married and started another tradition of Christmas Eve with my wife's family.

Develop a family mission statement

So much is made of mission statements these days in business life. In our private lives, we seldom pause long enough to identify what is important to us as individuals, much less as a family. My wife and I have very strong beliefs and values that we share. Years ago, we sat down and developed a Family Mission Statement that defines our common dream for our life as a family. I would encourage you to create your own. If you need help, read Steven Covey's book, <u>The Seven Habits of Highly Effective Families</u>. It will help guide you in developing one. We try to be true to ours everyday, our children understand it and live it as well.

The Wagner Family Mission Statement

*We are a loving family that nurtures each other
as well as our community of friends and family.
We enthusiastically share our life experiences.
We believe that love is unconditional and that trust and
respect are earned. We give thanks through meditation
and prayer and recognize all that we have been blessed
with. We value our health of mind, body, and spirit.
We nurture our minds with education, experiences,
and lifelong learning. We nurture our bodies with
exercise and by eating excellent foods. We nurture our
spirits by meditating, nurturing others, and expressing
our love for each other.*

- Daymakers at work -

I believe that anyone who has chosen to serve others is in an enviable position, if they approach what they do as a gift. I also believe that those who serve with the most sincerity possess what I call "servant's hearts." That is not to mean that we are in any way inferior to those we serve, but in a unique position to make their day.

What is your noble purpose in going to work? Does the company you work for have a noble purpose? Do your co-workers share in it? It is so much more fulfilling to work when you know that what you are doing is having a profound effect on someone else's day or life. How does what you do contribute to the world around you? Many times a noble purpose is articulated in a company mission statement. I have a theory on company mission statements. I believe that they should be "bumper sticker short", meaning you should be able to fit it on a bumper sticker. They should also be profound. By profound I mean simple, clear and meaningful. A company or organization only becomes successful when it encompasses profound values that translate into fact and feelings that employees can project and customers can embrace. At JUUT, our noble purpose, our reason for being, is simple.

We Serve and Replenish.

Our noble purpose and the reason we get out of bed in the morning, excited for the day ahead, is best defined by the fact that each day we serve around 4,000 guests in our salons, spas, and stores. By replenishing them, we create an amazing ripple effect in our communities. Imagine if we make our guest's day, then they go on to touch ten others in a similar way at work, home, etc. Now we have touched not just 4,000 people, but 40,000. Ready for this? That's over 14 million people a year! Our staff clearly understands this ripple effect and their role in it. It is why they do what they do. When I ask our staff why they work at JUUT, they tell me it's because of the mission, to serve and replenish. People don't lead, purpose does. Noble purpose is profound in its simplicity. It is the essence of why you do what you do, and why your company exists. You can have an incredible career as a Daymaker doing any type of job, as long as you serve others. Think of all the opportunities you have throughout the day to touch people. It's amazingly simple.

Being a hairstylist taught me that so many people are hungry for genuine relationships with others. With the fast pace of life that many people lead, they simply don't take the time to foster relationships outside their family and/or work environment. They miss out on important human connections. Everyone needs an ear to listen, a shoulder to cry on and someone with whom to share a genuine Daymaker smile, and to celebrate joys and accomplishments.

Whether it is with your hairstylist, mailman, neighbor or brother, we all need those genuine relationships to feel important and appreciated. So take the time to listen, and share with those who seek you out. Then, when you really need someone, they will be there for you.

I have had the opportunity to follow some of my clients' lives through high school, college, marriage, children, and also some of the more traumatic times. I cherish each of them and know I played some small role in many important events. I have traveled out of town to do hair for my clients' weddings when it wasn't about doing her hair; it was about sharing in the happiness of the day. I have had the unique privilege of clients sending me incredibly personal mementos that they wanted to share with me; videos of their wedding, pictures from trips, even footage of a childbirth!

Once, I was even asked if I would videotape one of my client's deliveries for her. I politely declined. It does go to show how connected people get with someone who has listened, cared and repeatedly made his or her day. It instills a trust level that flatters and inspires me.

- Daymaker Leader -

What do Daymaking and leadership have in common? I believe that it is critical to have the heart and intuition of a Daymaker regarding people in order to be a great leader today. Whether it is leader of a country or a charitable program, teacher or salon owner. The talents and skills that are required to lead are similar no matter the circumstance or group of people being led.

A critical piece of Daymaking in a leadership role is: don't wait until people do things exactly right before you praise them.

Acknowledge any improvement, no matter how small. A pat on the back from your boss always makes your day and keeps you motivated to do more. This was not a lesson that came easily to me. When I started to notice and appreciate the "small stuff", it produced big results.

On Boss's Day in 1994, a full-page ad appeared in USA Today. It was contracted and paid for by the employees of Southwest Airlines. It was addressed to Herb Kelleher, the company's CEO:

Thanks Herb,

For remembering every one of our names.
For supporting the Ronald McDonald House.
For helping load baggage on Thanksgiving.
For giving everyone a kiss (and we mean everyone).
For listening.
For running the only profitable major airline.
For singing at our holiday party.
For singing only once a year.
For letting us wear shorts and sneakers to work.
For golfing at the LUV classic with only one club.
For out-talking Sam Donaldson.
For riding your Harley Davidson into Southwest Headquarters.
For being a friend, not just a boss.
Happy Boss's Day from Each One of Your 16,000 Employees.

A display of affection like that occurs only when a leader has worked hard to connect with his or her people. It's important to let the boss know they're doing a good job when they are. Even the boss needs a pat on the back; it's lonely at the top.

Good leaders find ways to convince their staff members that they see them as either winners or potential winners. In all of my mentoring by other leaders, I felt that I was viewed as a winner. In many instances, this gave me the confidence to actually respond to a situation as a leader, not someone who was trying to become one.

50

Calvin Coolidge was invited to a dinner hosted by Dwight Morrow, the father of Anne Morrow Lindbergh. After Coolidge had excused himself for the evening, Morrow expressed his belief that Coolidge would make a good president. The others disagreed and a heated discussion ensued concerning Coolidge's qualifications. Those who didn't believe in his presidential potential felt he was too quiet and lacked charisma and personality. He just wasn't likable enough, they said.

Anne, then age six, spoke up. "I like him", she said. Displaying a finger with a bandage around it, she continued, "He was the only one at the party who asked about my sore finger, and that's why he would make a good president", said little Anne.

Anne made a good point. In order to lead, one has to have sincerity, a spirit of kindness and genuine concern for others.

Leadership has a lot to do with confidence and enthusiasm. You gain confidence from your own experiences, convictions, and other people's faith in your abilities. The best leaders aren't the ones with the most followers; they are the ones who create the most leaders. Leadership at JUUT is approached in this manner.

Our goal is to create relationships so strong with our clients that they become raving fans of JUUT who will recruit their friends and family to our business.

We have two customers, internal and external. The leadership team focuses their resources on the internal customer, our employees. Education, financial planning, goal setting, coaching, effective marketing and advertising and great environments are all resources that we provide to our employees. We are passionate about serving them so that they have all the tools, training, and attitude to serve and replenish our external customer, the client.

I ask our employees to share their wild ideas and we provide resources for them to experience as many as possible. Some of our employees want to buy a house, so we provide them with classes on buying their first home. Some want to go to Europe to study, so we arrange tours. Some want to open their own salon, so we teach classes on opening your own salon. This might seem idiotic, teaching your staff how to become your competition. I don't think so. We teach them the pros and the con's, the risks and the rewards and at the end of the day, most find that they enjoy being an employee of JUUT long term. Those who do decide to open a salon have a much better understanding of what it takes. I believe we have an "emotional bank account" open with these individuals. I teach them not to steal staff from ours or other businesses because it will come back around to them some day when they can least afford it. Some have left to open their own salons and have done so with great integrity.

Those who share their wild ideas put themselves at a great advantage over those who don't. One of our staff members had a wild idea that he wanted to do hair for Vogue magazine before his career was over. One day, about a year after he shared that with me, Vogue called. They were coming to Minneapolis to do a photo shoot and wanted me to do the hair. I told them I had someone else who could do it and assured them it would be great. I told the employee about the shoot and he couldn't believe his wild idea was going to come true. He did the shoot and it turned out great. The interesting thing was how many other employees were upset that they didn't get to do the shoot. I simply told them that I didn't know it was their wild idea. Had I known that's what their wild idea was, I would have considered them to do it too. Now I have so many people telling me about their wild ideas, you would not believe it.

My favorite wild idea has become helping others realize theirs. It is so rewarding. Remember the Audrey Hepburn saying, "If you ever need a helping hand, you'll find one at the end of your arm; as you get older you'll realize you have two. One for helping yourself and one for helping others." I think this is true of wild ideas.

I believe that when we have gone beyond our staff's needs and expectations, it allows them to serve the client in ways that are unique, unexpected, and genuine, with a great attitude about the company they represent. Clients want to do business with a company that takes care of its employees!

We solicit input from staff members because they know their job best. The closer you get to the front line, where most of the action occurs, the more employee input is necessary. At Juut, we provide our team members with a "How Are We Doing This Month?" survey.

They are given the opportunity to comment, make suggestions, gripe or praise all the various aspects of the company, (i.e. Marketing, Front Desk, Education, etc.) We have gotten very useful feedback and implemented great ideas from information we received from these surveys. It is important that all employees feel safe in making the suggestions and that none of the ideas they bring forth are stupid or not valued. Always ask an expert, they are your front line employees. That's where you'll get the real answers you can use to improve your organization.

We have around 400 employees who are totally passionate about the well being of each and every client and their experience at JUUT. Being a Daymaker is really quite simple; we are doing what we do for one reason, to make our client's day.

Each employee has the same opportunity to be a Daymaker whether they are booking appointments, cutting hair, or selling products. We can make our client's day in the way we serve them their tea. To us, customer service uplifts and replenishes the client with love and joy. What we do becomes second to why we do it.

What we do is a commodity. The heart and soul of why we do what we do distinguishes us and our brand, JUUT, from other businesses in our industry. A brand is simply a promise to the client. At JUUT, we serve and replenish. That is our promise!

CELEBRATING DAYMAKERS AT WORK

Pass the bouquet

Each week bring a bouquet of flowers to work and give it to someone who made your day recently. Then, the person who receives it passes it on the next day to someone who has made their day and so on. When the week is up, five people have been told in a beautiful, tangible way, thank you for making my day. Recognition is a great motivator.

Daymaker cards

We have cards in our break rooms so that staff members can fill them out to recognize someone who has made their day by helping out, complimenting them, etc. We post these cards on the bulletin board in the break room for everyone to see and read them in our team meetings as a way of recognizing the value of Daymaking in big and small ways at work.

We know each employee's favorite flower

Remember the analogy earlier that $1 spent on something unique is more valuable than a $50 gift of something ordinary? We have in each employee file what their favorite flower is. Periodically, we send a note of congratulations for a promotion, engagement, pregnancies, etc., as well as our sympathies for a loss of a loved one or an injury. Instead of sending them a bouquet, we send them one stem of their favorite flower. Imagine getting one beautiful, fragrant stem of freesia with a note vs. an average bouquet? It's a way to keep it more personal. That goes for other gifts as well. One employee might enjoy theatre tickets when another would prefer to go to the zoo with their kids. Keep it personal and unique to the individual.

55

Harmony Awards

Each year at JUUT, we have our Annual Summit. We recognize such things as high sales, anniversaries, etc. The most coveted awards are what we call the Harmony Awards. Each salon votes on an individual they work with who has brought the most harmony to the workplace that year. We compile the comments and recognize them in front of the whole company. The tears of joy, not only from the recipient, but their co-workers as well, are very moving. When you place value on such things as harmony in the work place, you tend to get more of it.

Volunteer!

Think of ways you could benefit a children's hospital

Either uplifting the child's day or doing something for their parents. We provide haircuts, manicures, foot massages, and other services for the children, as well as just hanging out with them. We provide the same services for the parents who have had their worlds turned upside down and are staying at the Ronald McDonald house in Minneapolis. What could you do for the parents? Mow their lawn, wash their car, or cook them dinner. There are all kinds of opportunities to make both the child's and the parent's day.

- The Daymaker Traveler -

Much of what I read about for my own business to succeed, are articles and books on other successful enterprises. One such business that I had been reading about for years was Southwest Airlines, and the job that Herb Kelleher, their CEO, had done with the company. I had no previous experience flying on their airline, so I had to try it for myself. I can tell you now that it's a great airline that has fun. There are no frills, except for the great staff, and the rates are very inexpensive.

I attended a conference in Orlando and had business the next day in New Orleans. I booked a flight on Southwest for this leg of my trip. I arrived at the airport and went to the gate where I was given a boarding card. I had never seen one of these before so I inquired about it. I learned that to speed up departures, they give no one a seat, but the earlier you arrive, the earlier you board. "Makes good sense," I thought. I boarded with a colleague of mine. We had our choice of seats in the middle and proceeded to get ready for our flight. The pilot got on the P.A. and said a few things that made us laugh, not the usual ho hum announcements which actually made it fun to taxi down the runway. So, here we were in coach seating, with no frills, having a great time because of the employees of this extraordinary airline. They made us feel not only appreciated, but also an important part of their day. What a great experience!

8 hours later…

New Orleans: Check in at curbside and the skycap tells us he is not checking for Minneapolis. We have to go inside. My colleague and I check in and find out our flight has been canceled and we will be going through Memphis instead. It will add another few hours to our trip. Too bad, but no problem, as long as we get home.

On our way to Memphis…

In first class, they hang your jacket if you like when you board. I was seated in the fourth row and took my jacket off to be hung by the flight attendant. I started to read a magazine and left the coat draped over my lap. I guess that by the time the flight attendant took my coat, I was so engrossed in my magazine that I didn't notice she had taken it. She looked back at me and snidely said; "You're welcome." I looked up and watched her make her way to the front shaking her head in disgust at me. A few minutes later she asked the gentlemen ahead of me if he would like anything to drink before taking off. He replied, "A glass of red wine please." She returned and he said, "Thank you." She replied, "Well thank you, not everyone is as considerate as you are", while looking back at me in the next row. What had I done wrong? I wondered. Then, the guy next to me said, "Man, she is brutal to you tonight."

Just then, it happened again. Here I was flying in from a hair show, all dressed in black with long crazy hair, flying first class to Memphis, when the same guy seated next to me asks if I'm a famous musician flying to Memphis to play on Beale Street. I replied, "No, I'm a Daymaker", and proceeded to tell him the story as I had fourteen years earlier on another flight. This time though, I could show him an example on the spot. When the same flight attendant came around again, I told her, "I'm sorry if I was inattentive during takeoff, I was in the middle of a really engaging article in my magazine. Could we start over by my telling you how much I appreciate you taking such good care of us this evening?" The look on her face spoke volumes as she gave me a very appreciative, somewhat sheepish smile. My fellow traveler got a lesson in how easy it is to make some one else's day. Hopefully, she learned something as well.

In the morning I arrived in New Orleans flying coach, with no assigned seat and no frills whatsoever on Southwest, and had the best flying experience of recent memory. I later board the major carrier in the Minneapolis/St. Paul area, flying first class to Memphis and I'm treated like a jerk. In the end however, I turned an unpleasant situation into a pleasant one, another key factor in being a Daymaker.

"ON THE ROAD" DAYMAKING

Offer an elderly person your first class seat

If you have the opportunity to fly first class, take this great opportunity to make someone's day. If I see an elderly person struggling and flying alone, I love to ask them to switch seats with me. It inspires the others in first class and the flight attendants to be generous with their day

Allow someone in line ahead of you

A fellow traveler with one bag would greatly appreciate your letting them ahead of you, your family and all twelve pieces of your luggage. It's also incredibly kind to let someone with a connecting flight jump ahead of you so they don't miss their next plane. Similarly, keep this in mind whenever you find yourself standing in any line.

Part Four

HARMONY

Love, Light, Joy & Abundance

Daymaker Spirits

My first true realization of death was my sister Michelle, who passed away when she was thirteen and I was twenty-two. She was born with what is referred to as a hole in her heart. When she was just a few months old, she was one of the youngest to survive open-heart surgery. She was an incredible kid. Her cup was always half full. She couldn't do the things other kids could do because of her condition, but she was always smiling. What a gift she had to be happy. She had surgeries every few years as her body grew. One day, when she was thirteen, she came home from school and told my mother she wasn't feeling good and went to lie down. My mother went to check on her a short time later to find her dead of cardiac arrest. I still cannot imagine those moments my mother endured, waiting for the ambulance, so helpless, alone with my sister. It hits me especially hard now, as a father. To endure the passing of a child must be one of the most difficult challenges life could deal a person.

I remember thinking such a strange thought over the next few days. I knew I was supposed to be grieving, and in a state of sorrow, yet I felt uplifted and fortunate at the same time. I felt fortunate because my sister had survived multiple surgeries that she was not supposed to survive. I remember thinking, "What if she had not survived her first operation?" I would not have known what it would have been like to have a sister at all. All my emotions I felt for her and my memories of her over the thirteen years that I knew her, came over me and made my heart full. Watching her celebrate her first birthday, when the odds were against it, helping her learn how to twirl a baton and march around the garage, and so many others, all of this would have escaped me had she passed away when the odds indicated she should have. Our family was blessed for thirteen years with an incredible little girl who had a spirit that had I not had the brief time with, my life would not be as full today.

For this I am grateful, and it makes it difficult for me to feel bad about her loss when we all gained so much by her presence. Don't get me wrong, I still think of her and miss her dearly, yet her spirit always brings a smile to my face and a joy to my heart. In thirteen short years, she did more to give people hope, grace, and dignity in life than many people who live well into old age.

I learned a life lesson recently about death that I really was not prepared for. My wife and I experienced a miscarriage with our third child. We went in for our ultrasound and there was no heartbeat. It obviously was a very difficult time for us emotionally.

We were not prepared for this. How do you explain this to your four-year-old daughter who is joyously expecting a new baby? Coco, our oldest daughter, is very intuitive, and on the way home from pre-school with Charlie the next day said, "Mommy, why do some babies die in their mommy's bellies?" My wife nearly ran off the road. That evening, we proceeded to tell our daughters that the baby that was in mommy's belly, decided not to come into our lives at this time. We explained that the baby would forever be their guardian angel and always be with our family. We are sure of this, and our daughters now know that they will never walk alone. I like to think of life as ever circulating, that spirits are all around us and that there is no coincidence in our coming into each other's lives. We choose our way into this world, learn our lessons and hopefully elevate our souls to the next dimension.

Surround Yourself with Great Teachers

I had a great uncle who lived into his nineties and at his funeral, his obituary card said, "Some people say that it's hell getting old, I was one of the lucky ones that got to." Live your life, share it with others, and be kind in every moment. If you do, getting old will be a pleasure. If you are younger, find an older friend who can be your teacher and vice versa. Mitch Albom had Morrie Schwartz as his teacher and wrote about his lessons in, Tuesdays with Morrie. We all learned from the wisdom imparted on Mitch during their visits together. I have a friend and a soulmate in Greta Freeman, a woman I first met as a client. She asked me a question when I was 26 years old that I will never forget. She asked "David, if you could have two words on your tombstone, what would they be?" I thought about it while I was cutting her hair and told her I would let her know on her next visit. I gave this some serious thought and found that I couldn't quite capture it in two words. On her next visit, she asked if I had found my two words and I had to tell her, "No, I couldn't find them." I asked her, "What are your two words?" She looked right at me, with this incredible knowing in her eyes. She said very simply and confidently, "I lived." I was so taken by her answer that on her next visit I asked her if I could borrow her two words. She and I have been best of friends for nearly twenty years now. I no longer cut hair, but we love to go out for lunch together whenever we get the chance. The lunches last for hours. Mitch Albom had Tuesdays with Morrie; I have the great pleasure of "Wednesdays with Greta." Whether it is a neighbor, client, or grandparent, we all have so much to share and gain from having profound relationships with people outside of our own generation. It's just as important for older people to befriend those much younger. Our society seems to miss this opportunity of fostering relationships with others across generation lines. Everyone would benefit from a Greta in his or her life.

The Daymaker Ripple Effect

I chose to take a break from my business to go to Hawaii. I have been resisting coming on these vacations all of my married life, as I am not much of a beach guy. I have found that the most beneficial virtue in marriage is compromise, so we have been going to Maui for years now. We stay in a small town of Paia, on the North Shore of Maui. It is a very unique little village. We have gotten to know several parts of the world over the years, but we prefer to go back to Paia. It is a small village and is as close to the sixties as I can imagine. The people here are natives, professional wind surfers, or people like us who just come for the small town feel of the area. It's really an amazing place where hitchhiking is still the mass transit of the day, everyone pulls over for each other. I picked someone up to give them a ride one day and I couldn't believe how long it had been. It felt safe, the right thing to do, and it made their day. Remember the old days? They're back in Paia.

We go to the Library on Thursdays to listen to native women read stories to the children. This is not a tourist deal, the women are reading to mainly native children, and ours benefit from it greatly. That they experience this type of diversity and culture is very important to us as parents, and suits our Mission Statement.

One of our favorite restaurants is Mama's Fish House. I was there one night, doing my writing, when a waitress came up after her shift, obviously not having a great day. She was contemplating having her favorite glass of wine at the end of her shift. She was hesitant, as she did not have as prosperous of a night as she would have liked. I asked what her favorite wine was and ordered a glass for her. She could not believe that a total stranger would do such a thing. I don't know that I have ever bought a glass of wine for a waiter or waitress who was not a genuine Daymaker. I knew that she was a Daymaker by watching her with her customers, fellow waiters, etc. She thanked me. I told her it was because she was a

Daymaker and about the book I was writing. Just then, a co-worker of hers joined us and she told him how I had made her day. They started talking about the corporate jobs they had given up on the mainland and the life they had in Paia, being Daymakers. They both had family back home that didn't quite understand why someone with a degree would want to wait tables in Maui. They both said they would now tell their families that they were Daymakers, not wait staff. They "got it", and I had a memorable evening with them. A few days later, Chris, the waiter, now a Daymaker, informed me that a waitress needed to leave early and that he was going to stay late and take her shift to make her day.

I received an e-mail from my friend Chris, the Daymaker, a few months later that inspired me to share our story and his poem with others.

"A message brought, begins to spread.
As through your words, old fears are shed.
For the thoughts of one will soon migrate,
when willing minds do congregate.
A joy in me does re-awake, when through my smile,
your day I make."
"Keep up the great work." - Chris!

Whoever or whatever your inspiration, it seems that by being a Daymaker, we all bring about the change in the world that we so long for. When each of us does our small part, and that ripple meets the other acts of kindness, there will truly be an awakening around our world. We will live long enough to experience this awakening. I know it. The sooner we get started, the sooner we can all experience that wave of kindness and compassion. The good old days are ahead of us, not behind us!

CONCLUSION

Hopes and Dreams

I feel awakened to the potential within our simple gestures towards others. When we look back on our lives and see we have touched so many people in positive ways and lead productive lives full of love and joy, we will be comforted, I am sure. If we cannot look back in this way, it will be very sad. What we experience is totally up to us. We cannot change the past and the mistakes we have made. What we can do is learn from them and make the most of each day. We all need love and happiness; we can have it through serving others.

I know this is my life's work. - To serve others and influence others to do the same. I feel like a Daymaker warrior. I am part of a revolution of inspired people who see the opportunity to change the world simply by being Daymakers.

Make your life extraordinary by being a Daymaker with everyone you touch. There is nothing mysterious about this. It is nothing more than acting out of concern for others. As you do this more and more, you will find that you gradually develop a habit of Daymaking in life. You will think less of your own needs and concerns and more of the impact you can have on another person's day. You will find a peace and happiness in yourself. One day it will be effortless and unconscious. It will be your essence, your being- ness, and your soul. Your life will be full of perfect moments.

I used to find myself sitting on the sidelines of life hoping the world around me would somehow become better. I have now realized that I must participate fully in my life and in my world to create the type of life I want; full of peace, compassion, humor, love, and an abundance of everything that's good, and right, and true.

I have knowledge that does not come from a formal education, as I do not have a doctorate or master's degree in the area called life, just many experiences that have taught me at my soul's level.

When I became still, I became aware. I am aware that there is a tipping point in any circumstance and that we are on the brink of one in the world today. I am also aware that I have a role, like you, in tipping it the right direction. Why settle for a world full of fear, loneliness, despair, and hate? We cannot sit on the sidelines and hope. Unfortunately, there are also forces pulling the opposite direction. I believe that a small group of people can change the world or I would not have written this book. I see it as a ripple effect, these good deeds, simply done in mundane and celebrated ways. I dream of a world for our children and our children's children in which this ripple has become a wave, and that it becomes so powerful that it washes away the unnecessary pain and suffering in the world. We can do this. I know it in my soul. I am full of hope, conviction, and confidence that there is a Guild of Daymakers in the world. They join me on this path of changing the little things in life everyday. We'll see that these little deposits will result in a very large shift in our society in our lifetime. It's already occurring all around us.

My hope, my dream is that people around me, as well as people around the world, might read this book and take big and small steps toward making someone's day. I believe that the world will change in my lifetime, and that it starts with me.

If it's to be, it's up to me.

If you feel that this book has touched you, I would ask you to pass it on to another Daymaker-in-the-waiting and continue the ripple effect.

Thank you for allowing me to share my life and dreams with you. I hope someday that we might meet and make each other's day.

David Wagner